THE ARTIST

A NOVEL

TILAK DHIMAN

To the 'Artist' who believes in dreams.

Contents

Contributors

Edited by Paula Shene/Tilak Dhiman
Layout by Tilak Dhiman/Paula Shene
Cover Design by Tilak Dhiman
Tea Luck Publishers
33 Locust Ave, Southampton, New York
tealuckpublishers@gmail.com

CHAPTER ONE

A Chance Encounter

"She may not come, maybe, she doesn't love me ... she doesn't love me at all, but..., but she had promised to come and meet me. Am I not good enough to be loved?" saying all this to himself, he stared at the withered rose in his hand, which was no longer fresh to tempt any lover.

That day once again she did not come. However, his heart was replete with hope and eyes still waiting for her. That day, he realized the truth about love - that love never ends, because at times it never begins. It was a little difficult for him to accept it, but it was true.

"Lonely hearts always need love and appreciation," he thought.

Then he looked all around, and realised that it was quite late and maybe he was right. After such a long wait, it was very late, indeed.

For some time, everything seemed futile. He wanted to forget everything. Even a wait of two years had given him nothing but he had somehow hoped this day would get him enough love for his entire life.

"People want to be loved for a long time because their entire life goes in waiting for love," he thought.

Then he stood up, took a deep sigh, stared at the wilted rose and threw it away. He now wanted to leave that place as soon as possible.

He came on the road and hailed a taxi; then got into it and left that place immediately.

It was a winter night so he closed the window glass and his eyes as well.

Supposedly, the most successful love stories of this world all begin in winter. But, for him, it was too cold to start. He was cursing his fate, as it had never been in his favour so far.

After going some distance, the driver felt some problem with the tyres. Stopping the taxi, he got out, checked the tyres, and then came to him.

"Get down! I'm not able to take you any further; one of the front tyres is punctured."

He got out of the taxi and looked all around. There were hardly any vehicles on the road at that time.

"Will you change it now?" he asked the driver.

"Well, no, I don't have any spare tyre right now," said the driver, showing his reluctance,

"You have to take another taxi."

"Can I get another one at the moment?"

"Don't worry," replied the driver, "Wait for some time, otherwise I'll manage another taxi for you."

After some time, a car seemed to be coming towards them. The driver was standing on the road.

Waving his hand he cried, "Stop, stop!"

The car stopped and he approached the front door of the car and asked the driver for help. The driver pointed to the back seat of the car.

An old man was sitting on the back seat.

"Sir, I need your help!" asked the driver and explained the whole matter to the old man.

After listening to him carefully, the old man gave a hasty look at the young man and smiled. Then he nodded his head saying yes.

Before sitting in the car, the young man paid the rent of the taxi and thanked the driver. Then he got into the car and they drove off.

The old man looked at the young man and smiled; the young man smiled too.

"What is your name?" asked the old man.

"Avi"

"What do you do?"

"I have just finished college and am looking for a job."

"Well, what sort of job are you looking for?"

"I don't know, but I have to do something quickly," he replied with a gentle smile.

"But you must have a direction. Without direction you can not achieve anything," said the old man showing his concern for the young man.

"Yes, that is true but finding a job is not my destination; I need a job just to strengthen myself financially."

"Where is your destination?" asked the old man.

"Well, I don't know exactly, but I want to write a book,"

"Very good!" replied the old man in an appreciative tone. "What would it be about?"

"It would be about life and love."

"That's great!"

"How old are you?"

"Twenty -five"

"I feel you are too young to write about such things,"

"I don't care. I just want to write," replied the young man in a determined tone.

"But, don't forget to give me a copy of your book when you get published," said the old man laughingly and then they both laughed at this.

"What do you do?" asked the young man.

"I am a painter."

"Wow! That's great."

"I am a great lover of this art"

"That's good", said the old man, "If you like it, then you must learn it."

"Life is like a school and we should learn everything that we want to."

The young man nodded his head and took a deep sigh.

"Are you comfortable?" asked the old man. He smiled and nodded his head saying,

"Yes, I am comfortable," and turned his face towards the window.

The old man put his hand on his shoulder and asked once again.

"Are you okay, young man?"

And, this time too, he gave the same answer. It was only his smile, which was making him look comfortable; otherwise, he was not. He somehow kept his smile on his face with the same effort.

When somebody smiles, his eyes smile first. The old man knew it. He looked at his face.

"What is the matter, young man?" he asked him, "You can tell me"

The old man was caring, loving and in spite of being a stranger, he was friendly.

The young man took a deep sigh, and in an instant, unleashed all his emotions into words.

Listening to him carefully the old man put his hand on his shoulder.

"Such is life, son!" said the old man, "You don't worry"

"You are a good boy. Can you stay in my cottage tonight?" he asked the young man.,

They looked at each other and the young man nodded his head.

After about forty minutes, the car entered the gate of a small cottage. Both of them got out of the car and entered the cottage. The cottage was small but beautiful.

"You sit down," said the old man and himself, moved into the next room. The young man put his bag on the floor and sat on one of the chairs.

The old man entered the room and gave him a glass of water

"Do you live alone here?" asked the young man, sipping the water, then placing the glass on the table.

"Yes, I am all alone here"

"So, you were going to your friend's home," he asked the young man.

"Yes."

"Forget her! And forget the whole incident just now", said the old man,

"Unrequited love always causes unhappiness in life".

"I can't, it is too difficult for me to forget her", said the young man.

"Look son, when someone loves you just love him, but when you love someone do not expect too much from him. You can't force somebody to love you in return. You can't make somebody love you", said the old man, making him understand the philosophy of love in life.

"This is what I have experienced in life and this is what I know about love.

Love is like a flow of emotions of your heart that flows from you to the heart of the person you love. If that person loves you, this flow will get reflected in you and if he doesn't love you ...it won't come back to you at all."

The young man looked concerned. He looked into his eyes.

For some time, there was silence in the room.

"Then what was wrong with my love?" asked the young man.

The old man looked at him, "Do you really love her?" he asked him.

"Yes, I do"

"How much?"

"Maybe ...more than I love myself."

The old man smiled and took a deep sigh. "Look son, nobody can love somebody more than he loves himself; it is absurd. Our selfishness always comes first and the rest of the things come thereafter."

"I didn't get you."

"Hmm...you are too young to understand this right now", said the old man.

"Then tell me what I can understand right now," asked the young man.

"Can you define love?" asked the old man.

"Love is very important in life; it plays a crucial role in building lifelong relations with people," said the young man.

"No, it's not right defination, son. Love does not do it alone. You need an unfathomable sense of adjustment to make strong and lifelong relationships in life," said the old man, "You can't rely only on love all your life, love is a belief that you will take care of your loved ones and you'll equally be taken care of by them."

"But ...in my case, where is the space for adjustments?" asked the young man in a curious tone.

"Love comes first and adjustments come later, your love is not developed as yet. It is still in the making. So do not talk of adjustments. Love can only be a root to begin a relationship but it cannot guarantee a good relationship. There are people who love each other so much that they get married, but after spending just a little time together, they cann't live together.

Then what is the role of love between them? Why do they separate? Asked the young man.

Love has no power to keep them together all their life. It is the sense of adjustment that keeps them together all their life. Love brings dependence into our life. When two people fall in love with each other, they start depending on each other. They need each other's presence in their life and start working for each other. This dependence and need for each other becomes the very soul of a good and perpetual relationship." Saying this, the old man looked at the wall-clock and stood up.

"What will you have for dinner?"

"Hm... nothing," the young man replied shyly.

"I'm going to the kitchen, you sit here comfortably," said the old man and then moved into the kitchen.

"You can see the books in the bookshelf," said the old man from the kitchen.

He got up and went up to the bookshelf. It was full of books.

He glanced through the bookshelf and picked up a few.

"You have got a huge collection. You seem to be a great lover of books,"

"Yeah, I read them when I get time. You can take a few."

The young man pulled a few books out of the rack, picked up one, and started leafing through it.

"This is one of my favourite books."

"Which one?" asked the old man.

"A roofless home."

"Yeah, it's a great piece of work," replied the old man from the kitchen.

"What sort of books do you like to read," the old man asked him again.

"I read novels, especially of Dostoyevsky. He is my favourite novelist. I have read almost all of his novels".

"That's good. If you want to be a writer, you must be an extensive reader. Read a lot, whatever you are interested in. Read and write on a regular basis." Saying this, the old man came out of the kitchen.

"Yeah, that's right." The young man said.

"What do you read barring Dostoyevsky?" Said the old man sitting beside him.

"Everything. Non fiction, spiritualism. I have a huge collection of Osho's books."

"That's great."

"Work hard, son. Do what you want to do in life. Our passion and enthusiasm decide our success. You will definitely achieve what you want to".

Saying this, the old man stood up and went to the kitchen again.

"Would you like to drink some tea?"

"No," replied the young man.

The old man came out with a cup of tea for himself, and sat beside him.

"I have a bad habit of drinking too much tea. I hope you don't mind."

The old man smiled and sipped the tea.

"Youngsters must have a proper vision in life. There is a lot of competition in this world. You must fight, but never waste your energy uselessly. Just preserve it for the right time and occasion. Read inspiring books. Meet good people."

CHAPTER TWO

Lessons Of Love And Life

The moon was in its full charm throwing its moonlight all around. The young man was standing by the window, witnessing the exquisite view of the night. He could feel the chilly night wind on his face. Therefore, he rubbed his palms together for a while, and put them on his face to feel some warmth.

He took a deep breath and with the same effort exhaled all his worries. He felt a touch on his shoulder, he looked back, the old man was standing behind him.

"I think you should go to bed now."

The young man looked into his eyes, "No, I'm not sleepy at all." The young man smiled and turned his face to the window.

"I'm enjoying the view; it's extremely beautiful. I want to understand the stillness of the night. I want to sit here for some time."

The old man smiled and then walked back to the door.

The next morning, the old man woke up early, did some prayers on the bed. After the prayers, he took his walking stick and peeped into the young man's room. The young man was still sleeping.

After some time, the old man entered the room with two cups of tea. He pushed the door. However, he pushed it very gently, but the squeaky door interrupted the young man's sleep. As soon as he saw the old man coming into the room, he got up and sat on the bed.

"Good morning son!"

"Very good morning" Replied the young man smilingly.

The old man gave him a cup of tea.

"I won't disturb you at all," saying this, the old man turned back to the door.

The young man took a sip of tea and then took a deep breath. He looked out of the window and could see the sparkling sun behind the trees. Everything was so beautiful.

He finished the tea, and went to the window. Now, he was feeling a little energetic.

Then he went to the bathroom, washed his face, and admired himself in the mirror.

His face did not have a frown. It was smiling now.

'Morning' is the beginning of a new day, the day of new hopes, the day of some new and beautiful thoughts. He was calm. He was feeling good. The old man's advice had lessened his worries.

The previous night had changed him completely. Now, he was desirous to know more about love. He was not familiar with love as yet. However, he was impressed with the old man's remarkable and remedial explanation of love. Now, he was interested to learn the lessons from the literature of love.

Yesterday he was rather despondent about love and life. But his meeting with the old man had changed him overnight.

"It is amazing," he thought.

He came out of the bathroom and went to the old man's room. His sight fell on a painting on the wall. It was of a woman having a smile on her face.

"Beautiful! what a painting!" the young man mumbled.

The old man came with some breakfast for the young man.

"Whose painting is this?" asked the young man.

The old man placed the breakfast on the table without saying anything.

"Who is she?" The young man asked him once again.

It was a little niggling for the old man, because it concerned his past. Moreover, he was not in a mood to talk about it. He gave a hasty look to the painting and then looked at the young man taking a long and deep breath.

"She is my wife."

"Your wife!"

"Yeah."

"Where is she now?"

"Maybe I'm not the nicest person to live with." The old man said in a very sad voice.

Then he went to the painting, stared at it for some time, and came back to the young man. Then, he sat down on the chair holding his walking stick tightly.

"She does not live with me, because I'm a failure in life." The old man said in a heartrending voice.

The young man looked at the old man's eyes. They were full of pain and anguish. They were full of tears and loneliness. They were full of an unfathomable silence. However, there was still some hope in them. They were all set to reveal the mystery of their existence. They were looking around for someone to understand the old man's melancholy and share the untold tale of his writhing heart.

The young man was very excited to know about the old man's love life.

Recalling his past, the old man started telling his evocative tale to the young man:

"When I was young, I used to write poems. Poetry was my greatest passion. I was very ambitious and wanted to be famous. My friends always encouraged me. They all gave me great support.

However, my father was not happy with my dream. He never appreciated me. He was a businessman. He had no time for other things except his work. He was always busy and wanted me to help him in the business too. However, I was busy in my own business and my business was to compose poetry.

My father always suppressed my dreams and I had to live with repressed desires. This caused relationship problems between us. His awkward behaviour instilled hatred in my heart for him.

However, despite all this I never allowed myself to be disrespectful towards him. After all, he was my father."

Saying all this, the old man paused for some time and took a deep breath.

It was not that easy for him to unveil his past. The old man remained silent for some time.

The young man was looking at his face.

The old man had become a little troubled by this time. Still, he kept his words flowing.

"Dreams never come true." He started again.

"They are just an illusion of mind. Despite being resourceful, sometimes we are not that successful in achieving things. Moreover, sometimes we are forced by circumstances to leave them. Therefore, I have a little suggestion for you, young man." The old man paused for a while.

"Don't dream unless you have the ability to make them a reality. Don't dream. Respect your dreams and generate the will in you to achieve them. Perhaps, I did not have the ability and strength. Perhaps, I did not have enough willpower to keep the fire of my talent burning. I could not turn my dreams into reality. I was a failure. I was a failure in my life. Moreover, this was the biggest disappointment of my life. I became a poet, but not a good poet." The old man said in a sad tone.

The young man was still staring at his face. He was lost in his story.

"But who did paint that?" The young man interrupted him.

This question pulled the old man out of his reverie.

"Oh! How stupid I am." The old man laughed and took a deep breath.

"I forgot to tell you about the painting, sorry!" The old man said laughingly.

"I was lost in my dreams." Then he started once again.

"My relationship with my father was not good. As time wore, it got worse. Moreover, one day I left home." The old man added.

"I was on the road. I was frustrated. I wandered around the streets to get some work and, in the course of my struggle I strived even to stay alive. That time was very difficult. I was mentally disturbed. Nevertheless, my destiny had brought this phase into my life. I persisted in my difficult times somehow. I tested my luck everywhere. By using all possible means, I tried to get myself a few resources. Eventually, fate turned it's heels and did a favour to me and I managed to get some work somewhere. I got a job in a restaurant. The struggle in my life had begun.

I just tried hard and held on there, somehow. Besides, doing work for a living, I started writing poetry again and persisted as hard as I could." The young man was listening very keenly.

"A difficult decision always provokes us to make some of the best efforts of our life. And that teaches us to take and live life with a certain mindset." The old man said further.

Then he paused for some time and took a deep breath to revive his sad voice, which had become a little tired because of the long conversation.

"During this time, I improved myself as a human being and groomed my poetic talents to a great extent," added the old man. I started composing poetry once again and became busy in producing many poems. By this time, I was a satiated and hardworking man. Moreover, this was the world I had always wanted to live in." The old man was completely lost in his nostalgic past. Perhaps, he was enjoying living it all over again.

"One day one of my friends, who was a painter and worked with me in the same restaurant, came to me and showed me two tickets of a painting exhibition, insisting me to accompany him. Being an introvert, I said no at first, but when he insisted, I agreed to go. Being an artistic man, I had great respect for artistic things so, I could not refuse him.

"When you have an artistic temperament, you get familiar with every art automatically. Our natural understanding gets us closer to every aspect of it, making us mature and capable to get across every aspect of every art. We need to remain in touch with art, no matter which form of art it is," said the old man, taking a short pause and then coughing.

At this, the young man went into the kitchen, brought a glass of water for the old man, and sat down giving it to him.

The old man took a sip of water and put the glass down on the table.

"Thanks," he said to the young man.

The young man smiled a little and said, "Don't worry, you just relax,"

When a volcano erupts, it is impossible to hold back the flow of lava from its mouth.

The same thing happens with us, when we become emotional; it is always very difficult to control our feelings," the old man said, starting once again.

"We went to the exhibition. When we entered, we were enthralled to see some beautiful paintings. Really, that was amazing. That was typical artistic work in front of us."

"My friend was very excited, and why not, even I was elated.

As we were busy admiring the great work, someone interrupted us.

"Excuse me!" A voice came from behind.

Turning back, we saw a girl standing behind us looking at a painting.

"do you like the painting?," she said to both of us.

"Yeah, of course! It's nicely painted," I said.

"Are you a painter too?" The girl asked me.

"No, I am not, but he is," I replied pointing at my friend.

Then she introduced herself to us.

"All these paintings are mine," she revealed excitedly.

We were surprised at her revelation.

"That is very good, nice meeting you," I said to her.

"Me too," she said smilingly.

In the meantime, my friend moved on to the next corner to see other paintings. However, we two kept our conversation going on for some time.

"You are a very good painter," I said to her.

"And you are a very good writer," she said to me

I was a little surprised at this.

"I have read some of your poems," she said.

"Thank you very much,' I said smilingly

I was a little surprised at her. A girl who I had never met before was talking to me in such a frank and friendly manner but I was enjoying it.

She looked at me. I looked at her and we smiled gently.

I admired her from head to toe. Her eyes were replete with temptation, her reddish- brown hair dangling to her hips. Her penetrating look was amazing. She was beautiful. Moreover, she was elegant. I was stunned. I had never ever seen any girl looking at me this way in my life. I was trembling.

"Nice talking to you," she said.

I pulled myself back to my previous position, shaking my head and blinking my eyes repeatedly.

"Pleasure...is all mine," I said smilingly.

"Nice girl," my friend said, teasing me.

Then we came out of the exhibition hall.

I forgot that incident very soon. I became busy with my life.

After a few days, someone knocked at my door. Opening the door, I looked out. I was stunned to see that girl standing in front of me.

I had never imagined meeting her in my house.

"Oh! ...you!" I said surprised, "Come in please."

Then she came inside and sat down comfortably.

"How did you find my house?" I asked her.

"I asked your friend," she replied in a quick attempt. Then she smiled gently. She had no hesitation in front of me. She was so sophisticated.

"It is a pleasure to see you in my house." I said hesitatingly. What would you like to have...Tea...Coffee ?"

"Nothing." She said, "I will not waste your time. Actually, I want to see your poems. I want to read them," she said." May I see them? I will not waste your time." she asked me.

"Sure, why not?" I said smiling.

I went to my room, brought out the diary of my poems, and gave it to her. She took it from me and started browsing through it.

"May I take this with me?" she asked me "I will return it later."

"Hmm...hmm...sure." I thought for a moment or two and gave the diary to her.

"You can stay here for some time." I insisted.

"Hm...hm...no, I have to go now," she thought for a while and refused my offer.

"All right," I said.

Then I escorted her to the door. She turned back, smiled once again.

"Good bye," she said, "we will meet soon."

"Yeah... we surely will," I said.

Then she went out and I closed the door.

We met several times thereafter and every time, I felt a very strong feeling of love for her.

After some time, she shifted to some other city, which was very famous for the art of painting at that time. One day she came back to me.

"I am leaving this city," she said. I want you to be with me."

I thought for some time and said, "All right, I will go with you."

Then after a few days, we shifted to that city. Life can not be the same all the time. However, sometimes, we can only expect it to be that way.

She became busy in the world of painting. On the other hand, I forgot my world of writing. I now wanted to marry her. Several times, I asked her to get married and every time she said "We will, soon."

Moreover, I had lost my interest in writing poetry. One day I forced her to give me clarity on our marriage.

She smiled indifferently, "I do not have time yet... really," she said, I need to go a long way as yet, I have other things to think about yet. I can not marry you. I do not want to ruin my career. My dreams are more important to me than marriage."

I was shocked. I could not easily get what that meant. However, whatever she said was very hurtful.

"How can she say that?" I thought for a moment. A woman to whom I was ready to devote my entire life, had no time for me? A woman for whom I had even forgotten my dreams, was asking me to forget her? A woman for whom I had left everything, wanted to leave me?"

Saying this, the old man took a deep breath. Maybe, he wanted to say more but, his pain prevented him from saying anything, thought the young man.

"Why did she say that?" asked the young man.

"I never understood," the old man replied. I was going to give up my writing to give her time and she was ready to leave me to give all her time to painting. She had no hesitation on her face while saying all this to me. I was not a suitable companion for her, and maybe, she was not my true love.

But I learnt one thing from that incident."

"What was that? The young man asked him.

"Being over ambitious destroys us. A dreamy woman can never love you to that intensity; she can not love you at all. She will be insensitive. She will kill your sensitivity, because she knows nothing about love. She can never respect your feelings. Moreover, she will not have much time for you."

Saying this, the old man coughed for a while and took a deep breath. The young man was lost in the story. He forgot to even blink his eyes.

"Love and dreams can never go simultaneously, " the old man started once again. Love arises from the heart, whereas dreams come from the mind. The heart is tender, whereas the mind is very aggressive. And in the battle of these two, the mind always wins," the old man explained.

"Always remember son!" the old man said. The young man started looking at him more curiously.

"Opt for only one thing in life, either love or dreams. Never mix them up, else, you will perish," the old man said.

"But, sir," the young man asked him, are not both complementary to each other?

"Yes, they are," the old man replied, making him understand. Dreams give us momentary happiness, whereas, love is not a momentary happiness. It is a matter of joy forever. Dreams are a strong urge that forces us to attain materialistic pleasure in our life. Whereas, love inspires more than it forces."

The old man paused for a moment.

"You were asking me about that painting. That is of that girl. My friend painted it for me," the old man said looking at the painting.

The young man wanted to ask something but the old man stopped him.

"Do you remember?." the old man asked once again, when you entered my house, you asked me whether I was alone and I answered, "I am here but not alone. This is because I live with my poems. They are always with me and will always be here. But there is one thing I do not usually do."

"What is that?" asked the young man.

"I do not have dreams now. I do not dream any more. They ruined me. They spoilt my whole life."

"How sad!" the young man said, taking a deep breath. "It had everything: trust, love, attraction, devotion, dreams and betrayal too. A story with a good beginning but, unfortunately it fizzled out in the end. Both have been unfair to you."

"Both?" the old man asked him.

"I mean life and love," the young man replied.

"Despite all this, I have no regrets against God," the old man said.

I accept his decision. It had to happen. I am happy as ever."

"You are great!" the young man said. I have never ever seen a brave man like you. Despite all this you have no complaints in life. And how foolish I am, replete with regrets and complaints in my life," the young man added.

"I was crying over a story which was not mine. I had no sense of judgment; everything had gone wrong just because of me. Now I have understood that I had no sense of love and life at all. You have lost so much. You are now replete with anguish and melancholy; still there is always a smile on your face. Still, you are meek and calm."

Looking at him the old man smiled without saying anything. Both looked at each other. The young man's eyes were full of questions, whereas, the old man was ready to answer them all.

"Did she never meet you thereafter?" the young man asked once again.

"No, those who run after dreams never care for others," the old man replied sensibly. She was busy in her world and I came back here. I never tried to approach her thereafter.

"Did she never stop you from breaking this relationship? the young man asked again.

"Yes, she did, but I think she knew my determination and moreover, her fault as well."

"Do you still love her?" the young man asked him straightaway.

"Yes, I do and I always will," the old man replied. I have been inexpressive all my life. But there is nothing to be expressive about now."

The young man seemed to have nothing to ask after that. Both remained silent for a while. However, that very moment seemed to be expressive.

The old man took a deep breath and said, "Young man, life is full of colours. And if love is there it becomes beautiful and supportive."

Having said all this the old man stood up with the help of his walking stick and went to the next room.

The young man was still thinking of him and about the story, he just told him. He was extremely impressed by the old man's philosophy of love and life. Just because of the old man, he had learnt a few lessons of life.

After some time the old man came to him with a diary in his hand and gave it to him.

"Young man, this diary contains all the poems I wrote for her living in this cottage.

The young man took the diary and opened the first page. Following was the first poem that he read:

Darling...darling, little wait,
Tell me is this love or hate?
Now, turn is mine, let me play,
You have said, let me say.
Love is blind; love is fine,
I am yours; you are mine.
Without you, I will suffocate.
Tell me is this love or hate?
You are my heart. You are my soul.
You are my fate. You are my goal.
I cannot live. I cannot die.
I cannot smile. I cannot cry.
Do not break my heart, it is delicate.
Tell me is this love or hate?
What to do, I do not know.
What am I, I do not know.
I just know you are mine,
You are my Sun, you are my shine.
Love me now, do not hesitate.
Tell me is this love or hate?
My love is clear, my feelings are pure.
My heartbeat is down, only you can cure.
My day is black; you are getting bright,
Maybe I am wrong, maybe you are right.
Come on soon, it will be very late,
Tell me is this love or hate?
I was looking there, but I was not scared,
You even came to me but, never cared,
I fell in love; I do not know why?

You broke my heart; I do not know why?
You always smiled having lots of hate.
Tell me is this love or hate?
Love is little, having a long wait,
If such is life then why to wait,
...Tell me is this love or hate?

"Wow! This is too good," the young man said after reading the first poem. Without reading any further, he closed the diary and put it on the table.

"Life is too brutal," the young man said again. A man, who dreamt big dreams, tried his best to turn his dreams into reality, a man who renounced everything for love in life, got nothing in the end, except a solitary cottage and a melancholic life. But he is still living smilingly."

The old man looked at him. There was silence for some time. Then the old man smiled and said, "Life teaches us everything, young man. What we learn from life becomes our experience. It is not wisdom but experience."

Saying this, the old man paused for a moment and took a deep breath. They were so engrossed in talking to each other.

CHAPTER THREE

A New Journey

The young man said good-bye to the old man and set off on a new journey. His mind had now completely changed. After walking some miles, he felt tired. He saw a tree and sat down under its shade. After walking a little, he saw a man squatting in the middle of the road. At first, he did not pay much attention to him. However, it seemed a little unusual to him. He wanted to know what the man was doing. He got up and went up to him. He stood beside him for a while without interrupting him. The young man observed him carefully. He was surprised at that man. He was picking up earthworms and putting them in the grass nearby. Moreover, he was doing it very gently and carefully. He stood there for some time. When his curiosity became uncontrollable, he asked him.

"What are you doing gentleman?"

The man turned back, looked at him without pausing his activity. Not getting any response the young man asked him again.

"Why are you doing this?"

This time the young man gave a hasty look at him and said,

"I am doing my duty."

The young man was very surprised at this strange answer.

"Duty!" the young man said. "What sort of duty is this?"

"God wants me to do this," He replied.

"God wants you to do it!" The young man was surprised.

"You are removing earthworms off the road. Did God say this to you?"

"Yes, He did," answered the man.

"Are you removing them off the road or collecting them," The young man asked him once again.

"I am not collecting them at all," he said.

"Then what are you doing?" asked the young man.

"I am just removing them off the road."

"Why are you doing this?" asked the young man.

"I am just helping them survive," replied the man. "I am just helping them to live on."

After some time, he stood up, looked at the sky, and swung around to the young man.

"How do you save their life?" The young man asked him.

"Either some vehicle will mow them down or they will get crushed under someone's feet," replied the man. "Therefore, I am removing them from the road and leaving them on the grass."

The young man was surprised at his answer.

"My goodness!" the young man mumbled. "You are amazing. How many people in this world think like you? People kill each other in this world and you are saving these helpless and crippling creatures here! You are too good."

The man smiled and looked into his eyes.

"They too have life like us, and this is a small effort to help them live a little longer," said the man.

"I am impressed with your kindness," the young man said. "God created the universe so generously; but people are selfish and ruthless. We always meet cruel people and sometimes happen to meet some good ones like you. God himself has scuffed up his omnipresence."

The young man took a deep breath and looked at the sky. He had become grouchy. His heart was now full of grudge against selfish people. However, on the other hand, he praised the man for his goodness.

"I learnt all this from the monks," the man said.

"Monks are usually very kind. They are very sensitive to life. They have a great regard for life. They say, "Life is like a gift for human beings. It is very precious."

The young man was listening to him very attentively. A sudden urge to know more about monks rose within him. He was so impressed with that incident that he decided then and there to be a monk.

"Where do you live gentleman?" asked the young man. Can you take me to the monastery? The young man asked him.

"I live in the monastery," the man said pointing towards it with his right hand.

"I want to visit the monastery with you gentleman." The young man told him.

"All right", the man said, "let's go."

After some time, they reached the monastery. It was the first time the young man had visited a place like that. He had never visited a monastery before. He saw the monks, with shaved heads wandering around. They wore maroon dresses. Some were doing prayers inside the temple. Others were busy counting their beads and chanting calmly. It was really a new experience for him. Everyone in the monastery looked disciplined and satisfied. They were all very religious but happy and devoted. The environment there was very soothing and peaceful. They entered inside and sat in a corner watching the activity of the monks. After sometime a monk came to them.

"Who are who?" the monk asked.

"I want to meet your guru," the young man said.

He took them to a room. They entered inside. The guru was in deep meditation.

"You sit here," the monk said. "Guruji is in meditation now, I can not interrupt him. You have to wait."

Saying this, he left the room. They sat down comfortably. The young man looked all around the room. There was nothing in the room except three people. The young man looked at the guru's face. His eyes were closed. Only his nostrils were moving in and out. The face was rather lute but calm. His body was so still, even a dead body could not be like that. The room was extremely serene.

After a long time, the guru opened his eyes. He took some time to get used to the room. His penetrating gaze fell on them. He blinked his eyes and smiled to see them. The young man leaned forward, at the guru's feet, to seek his blessings. The guru put his hand on his shoulders and tried to raise him up.

"Who are you, young man?" The Guru asked him in a soft voice.

The young man raised himself up to his previous position. Then he told the guru all about himself including the old man. The guru was listening to him carefully.

"I am here to present my services at your holy feet," The young man said.

"Not in my feet, son! In the feet of God," the guru said smilingly.

"I want to know God," the young man said.

"Holy God! Holy God! Holy are all the things,

He has bound all of us with his holy strings." the Guru said smilingly.

"God gives and we take. Nobody can obstruct your way without his consent. If you strongly desire and fairly deserve, God will definitely shower his blessings upon you, son! Life is a gift and you have to go through it. There is no other method to attain the experience of life. Before having some knowledge, you have to confirm your faith in God. If you are ready then remember one thing. He is the biggest resource of everything. If you are all ready to get it, you have to become the very path through which every experience will come to you automatically."

Saying this, the Guru became silent. The young man was silent too, only their heartbeats were saying something.

"The young man nodded his head and said," Yes, I will."

The young man stood there for a long time understanding the environment and his own self.

****

The young man had begun his journey to an entirely new world. One day he went to the guru. He entered the room the guru was meditating. The young man went to a corner and sat down comfortably. After some time, the guru opened his eyes and smiled to see the young man.

"I will tell you from the very beginning today," The guru said. Then he started the first discourse for the young man.

"Who is a seeker, do you know?" The guru asked the young man.

"No, I do not know," the young man replied.

"The seeker is one who is ready to know his own self," the guru said. "Who has dropped his worldly pleasures and longings. The one who has realized that to know himself is to know God."

The guru paused for some. time and took a deep breath. The young man was listening to him attentively.

"Love is the very first phase which begins life." The guru started once again. "It is the prime source which begets life. Then there come dreams. Whatever we do in life is because of dreams, longings, and needs. Our dreams and needs are responsible for our achievements, failures, sorrow, and happiness in life. This is the decisive phase of our life. We all pass through it. Love, desires, sufferings, happiness. This is all about life and this is called life experience."

"Is this life?" The young man asked the guru, raising his eyebrows.

"Yes, these all together make life," the guru said smilingly.

"How is love responsible to start life?" The young man asked the guru.

The guru was pleased with his curiosity and attentiveness.

"Yes, love is the very first phase of life," The guru added. "When two individuals get together, they attract each other, fall in love, mating happens.

It starts another life. Love comes into being, reproduction happens and another life begins. Now our needs and desires come to play their role in our life. Our desires and needs are the foundation of our sufferings and happiness. Now when we desire something in life, we try to obtain that. The efforts we exert in obtaining materialistic things in life take almost our entire life and we hardly reach our destination despite that."

"Are not love and desires two relevant forms of the same thing?" The young man asked him.

"No, there is a big difference between these two. Desires are endless. We are never satisfied in this world. We desire everything. However, actually, we need a few things in life to survive and we can not understand this. However, love is not a desire; it is a need. When there is no love, hate comes into being. On the other hand, hate is just the absence of love. Love is actually a search for solace. Whereas, desires are like a large hanky we want to keep in our pocket but we can not. Desires are just an internal kerfuffle for collecting things somehow."

The young man was satisfied with all this. However, he was looking to get a little more from the guru.

"When does the phase of suffering arrive in life?" The young man asked the guru.

The guru was expecting him to ask more so he replied immediately. "Sufferings are not alone; they come with happiness. They can not exist without each other. Sufferings and happiness do not come, they happen."

The young man was pleased to know all this. He breathed and tried to arrange his words for the next question.

"It is said that beautiful things are always innocuous. Then, why does love cause suffering?"

The guru was very calm. He knew that the ripples of curiosity had started arising in his mind. He smiled, looked at him and started explaining.

"Who says love has suffering!" the guru added up, "there is nothing as serene as love in this whole world. Love is always constructive. Sufferings are never situated with love. Sufferings come when we do not get the desired result, when we do not have predetermined results. This is a mere construct of our mind actually."

The young man was silent and calm now. He asked another question immediately.

"What is happiness?"

The guru looked at him and smiled at his innocence.

“Happiness is not about being happy all the time,” the guru began again. “Happiness is right there where you are satisfied in life. It is a state of mind when all your desires vanish.”

CHAPTER FOUR

The Revelation

The young man spent some years in the monastery. He had received a huge amount of knowledge. Time passed rather quickly. He had become familiar with the monks and their community. The most amazing thing was that now he was more familiar with his own self. He had a deep understanding of life now. He was much more confident about himself. He had no desire left in him.

One day he was sitting down with the guru. The guru was telling him something. He noticed that the young man was not as eager as he used to be before. The young man was not asking any questions that day. The guru showed his concern and asked the young man.

"What is the matter ...son?" The guru asked him. "Tell me right now."

"I...am..m.." he seemed to be a little uncertain.

Taking a deep breath, he looked at the sky and smiled as if to say, "I have understood everything now."

He had spent a long time in the monastery but the old man was still alive somewhere in his heart. He remembered the old man. He got up, went to the room and brought a diary with him.

He opened it and started reading a love poem:

Love is this, love is that,

Love is round, love is flat.
Love is earth, love is sky,
Love is deep, love is high.
Love is mind, love is heart,
Love is whole, love is part.
Love is day, love is night,
Love is black, love is white.
Love is here, love is there,
Love is far, love is near.
Love is little, love is long,
Love is life, love is song.

He turned every page carefully. The diary was full of some virtuous poems. The old man's life was very similar to this poem, little high, little deep, little bright but was bleak in the end. Love can change everything.

The young man could not control his emotions. He went to the guru and told him the entire story of the old man.

After listening to him carefully, the guru was stunned for a while. He took the diary and read a few poems.

"It is unbelievable!" The guru said. "May God bless him." Saying this, the guru became silent.

"I feel very sad for that man," the guru added.

Do you have any idea who that old man is?" The guru asked the young man.

"No, I do not have any idea," The young man replied.

"He was my friend," The guru told him.

"Do you know who I am?" The guru asked him again.

"No, I do not know," the young man replied, surprised.

"I am the painter, son! The guru cried.

The young man was stunned at this. The young man took a deep breath and looked at the sky.

"Love is beautiful but always encrusted with uncertainties. It makes us fall down and sometimes raises us high, but it always causes something. It is always involved in our life as a part of our life," the young man thought.

"Sometimes smiles, sometimes cries,
But it is a healing for woeful eyes,
Reviving the soul, it makes us alive,
It always is... it never dies."

9 798886 672473

Printed by Libri Plureos GmbH in Hamburg,
Germany